I0155350

to the god of sore feet and bad backs

poems by

Reverie Koniecki

Finishing Line Press
Georgetown, Kentucky

to the god of sore feet
and bad backs

Publisher: Leah Huete de Maines
Editor: Christen Kincaid
Cover Art: Taylor Teachout
Author Photo: Paul Koniecki
Cover Design: Elizabeth Maines McCleavy

Order online: www.finishinglinepress.com
            also available on amazon.com

Author inquiries and mail orders:
Finishing Line Press
PO Box 1626
Georgetown, Kentucky 40324
USA

Table of Contents

for all the bills i can't pay

miles ago my thighs
curdled into barbed wire

chain links wrap around
my flesh like nylon

I search for quarters
in the frozen food aisle

hands shake as I pass a bad check
bad as in it don't listen to its mama

bad as in spoiled, past its prime
bad as in it don't follow nobody

bad as in bad ass
bad as in a boomerang for brokenness

I wait for judgement and
wonder if there is a commandment

against having bad credit
the refrigerator is empty

the cashier gives me a receipt
for my lies

the shelf life of a promise
has the sharpest white teeth

with a cavity so hollow it sings
a loneliness so big it swallows

the children are watching
with black hole eyes

whole galaxies have succumbed
to another's wanting

the power of a debit card
with a positive balance

I unpack the groceries
blood before bread I say

1

God's intended garden

They say that boy had the devil in im'. Say he was Bad. Started as a cloud of disturbed earth. A horse blacker than night charging from cane fields with forces greater than Lazarus's reconstituted dreams. The only light, harvest moon eyes. No one dared move. Everyone, except for the boy, was afraid. You have to be careful Down South. The devil once had wings.

Cousin Mutley and I ask have never been Down South or seen the devil. We ask each other, do you want to go Up? Pointer finger toward the sky where God tends from cumulous clouds. Or Down? Pointer swivels to Earth's infected core. We wordplay by adding North and South to our questions. Follow up with mocking oohs that start low and rise with an unsteady soprano of innocence.

Nanny and Gramps are on knees beside their bed. Spirit starts as a cloud of disturbed breath. When Spirit enters your body, you speak Tongues. Heads bow. Hands pray. It's dusk. Lights are out. Candles burn on the dresser. Pastor Ella Beth praises God. Rubs holy oil on their foreheads. Spirit moves. Tongues lunge from depths of molars. Spirit fills room. Nanny and Gramps rise to unsteady soprano of innocence. Tongues are the language of God.

It started as a cloud of disturbed earth. Up North, God weathervanes his pointer. Horse blacker than night erupts from the thick of sweetness with the force of Gramps' stage 4 prostate cancer. Wounded animals escape diaphragms. Down South, the devil speaks Tongues.

They say that boy had the devil in im'. Say it was bad. Started with a cloud of disturbed earth. A horse blacker than night. A boy yielding to body. He mounts his horse. Spirit moves. Rides into cane fields. Spirit fills air.

This is God's intended garden.

Curbside Deliverance

My mother taught me to dream
by replacing my arms with wanting,

flipping through catalogues.
decorating the mansions I have yet to buy,

cutting out pictures of baby dolls with silken hair.
JC Penney and Sears are the gods

of too much and too many.
As in of too many seconds

and not enough breath.
As in, your dreams are the galaxy of

busted capillaries behind your eyelids.
When the weight of a man is infinity,

you call for your mother.
When the hunger of a man is infinity,

you call for your mother.
Your shoulder turns navels into eyes

into neck bones into knees into knee jerks
into asphalt into videos we can't forget

into none of us can breathe.
I used to run my fingers through the buttons

in my grandmother's cookie tin,
and see my future refracted

in the polychromatic chips of plastic.
Your future is two syllables

too heavy to carry alone.
When I ran up my first credit card,

I sat on the bill collector's lap
and told him what I wanted for Christmas.

The flower goes bad, when the stem is cut.
Your body pressed between avenue and tread.

Embers spill onto the street like milk,
like all the lives that do not matter.

When there is nothing left but dark matter
you call for your mother

Blessed be the weary who are tired of waiting.
You will never again clear your throat,

or touch the stubble on your jawline,
or rub sleep out of your eyes,

or feel how easy it is
to mortar bones to sand.

The Imagination of Resemblance

We pull over and park on that side street
just off of the Berlin Turnpike and follow

the trail to the ledge overlooking 91.
Windswept trees sway like lit matches.

Mosquitoes feast on our welted legs.
We rake skin with ragged fingernails.

We are red-fire-ant hot.
We are so electric,

we should be waterproof
We thought love was waiting for the city

to get around to filling the potholes
and watching headlights cast small fires.

The active construction zone blinds us.
We lay on our backs and watch the broken rib

of the night cleave the sky.
We couldn't tell the difference

between reflection or shadow
We melted like drugstore eyeliner.

but that was never the purpose.
We expected it to be easy.

Like that winter he worked at Strawberries
and turned off the alarm so we could steal CDs.

He says I love you,
and I want to break all the windshields.

The heat has broken righteously.
We speak in crashing waves

allowing words to carelessly lap the surface.
I pan for gold with cupped hands.

You paddle traffic,
we cradle the current together,

positioning ourselves toward the mouth,
toward the teeth we pointed,

the razors we uttered,
the arteries we severed.

disobeying gravity

now if there is no door to slam
nor house to hinge its spine
if these walls grow frameless
who will answer all of my names
vultures sitting on top of street lamps
waiting for someone to love them
enough to kill for them
neither headlamp nor confession
they breakfast and forgive
there are no vertebrae without hierarchy
lungs are tithing baskets leaping
over moving silence
the risk of reassembling glass
doesn't deter me from trying
nostalgia is a romance with a cigarette

Shopping

after the signs demand
she justify her innocence
no hoodies no backpacks
only 2 at a time allowed inside
she zips her purse shut
before she enters keeps
her hands close to her body
she sees a dress she wants
keeps it on the hanger
holds it arm's length away
all the way to the dressing
room the clerk tallies her
she carefully slips on
the dress that is not hers
onto this body that is
not hers the mirror reminds
her that her hip to waist ratio
is unexpected she
hands the clerk the wrong size
grabs a large and pays

the honeycomb of all things holy

glass notes waver in and out of silence
you tell me your mother was a saint
winding curiosity trickles like music
a ticking question ribbons the staircase
a helical tongue with no banister

faith is violent waiver
because every city must fall
the wide green palms of the fig tree
the wingspan of our eyes grazing the periphery

I want is a complete sentence
the unbalanced swing trying
the umbilical cord of desire
breathing is a privilege
you snore obliviously

I count your transgressions
on fingers stained with cheetos
the metallic bag crinkles
the cats come running

we are hungry
for white underwear
carrots and peas for supper
Slippers and bathrobe
a job with good benefits
a house in a gated neighborhood
vacations on the shore
brown ocean and shark piers
greasy restaurants overpriced trinkets
the unrelenting taste of salt

feet rooted in the ground
you branch into words
the mornings you feel closest to god
you feel most ordinary

When your oldest daughter gets mono,

You make apple ginger tea in the crockpot. You ruminate about the health properties of cinnamon and fresh ginger. How they're supposed to be the cure-all for everything. How the vitamin c from the freshly cut apples and limes will surely boost her immune system. You stir and think about how last night was the first time in years she'd asked you for a massage. And how surprised you were to discover that she still has that dry patch of raised skin on her left ankle. And how automatically your fingers travelled back in time to when you first brought her home from the hospital to that tiny two bedroom apartment in N. Ames Street. You are surprised that you still remember the detail of the pink-flower-swirling-green-stem-wallpaper. The green cushioned rocker and its matching moving ottoman that you'd put together yourself. You are surprised at how much your body aches for the absence of hers, how time has cleaved your bodies further and further apart.

This is the peninsula that broke off and became an island;

you think of the first time your mother drove you over the Chesapeake Bay Bridge as you knead her elongated legs. You wonder if she'll have more mercy than you, who just stood there in the lobby of Davidson Hall for a nanosecond before offering your mother a pageant wave and rising to the fourth floor where you would bloom into a freshman. You wonder if she'll allow you to cradle her one last time, If she'll pretend to not be embarrassed at your sentimentality. You roll your thumbs over the birthmark on her back. You remember how you used to give her lavender baths in the sink. You want to lift her. To accordion those arms and legs so she fits into your lap again. You want to hold her head fast to your chest as if both of your lives depend on this contact. You want to rock her till she falls asleep. To listen to each breath. You want to believe that each collapse of her chest will be followed by a subsequent rise.

a man left alone on a mountain gets billed for his rescue
for Kalief Browder

2 YEARS
the years you learn to whisper
talking through those vents
you are not alone
dirty cell as my witness
walls sweating w/o conviction
falling & begging for bread
mothers can't even help
it was always the hunger

3 YEARS
you no longer like to be touched
before release
after routine midnights

5 TIMES
you try not to breathe
but the teeth-sliced sheets
around your neck
hold onto you for dear life

20-25 MINUTES
your vent becomes an accomplice
your vehicle becomes a caprice classic
slats have holes
holes have opportunities

10 SECONDS
after you secure your noose
after the guard cuts you down
he hugs you with his arms
kisses you with his fists and feet
saving you only to kill you all over again

3 DEPOSITIONS/5 HOURS
they say you are faking it
they ask why you want to die
they don't know that you have a plan
light fixtures ceilings vent holes
are tools for target practice

11 ATTORNEYS
said you were invisible
turning you down
like a middle school girl
who circles the word *no*
on the folded lined paper
you've just passed to her
as if not being seen
is synonymous with guilt

12 X 7 FOOT
cell
locked

15 YEARS
an offer that can't be refused
waiting to pee
in line at the urinal
you pray

16 YEARS
you are a good kid

23 HOURS
Like Henry "Box" Brown
you package yourself
to freedom

30 COURT DATES
and your debt is not tabulated
your mother helps you calculate
the distance between swings
and balances you on her shoulders
like a trapeze artist
you flip

3 YEARS
a window slides open
as if welcoming you to buy fruit
the guards unfold your hands
the box abducts your flightless bones

15 DAYS
after your last interview
your incisors bite you again

to the god of sore feet and bad backs

blessed are these calloused hands
for they shall inherit the rent

zebras don't just climb out of the belly of the lion
empty cabinets don't just overflow with cast iron

if only hunting your enemies was as easy
as sliding an insult across a table

if only instinct was as keen as an empty stomach
when i wash my feet i call myself a disciple

a triangle is only a triangle on paper
its mouth may be closed but in the crook

of its elbow lies the answer to every angle
which proves nothing

Trouble swallowing

the street is thick with ticking motors
seeping into unwanted spaces
the shoulder drops off into
brother vs. brother reconstruction
this will not kill you

when you receive your diagnosis
allow your tongue to stumble
until you mispronounce it smoothly
this will not kill you

when the body betrays itself
assign it a nickname
split it in half call it a nation
call an undeclared war
keep smiling
this will not kill you

this will not make you stronger
this will not make your hair grow
six inches in one month
this will not make your credit good

this will not cure you
but you will continue to pump gas
long after the engine has blown

Labor Day

The last Friday of August,
the town's annual white-hooded

visitors came, dragging their crosses.
We white knuckled the grocery cart

while my mother bought enough rations
to keep us inside until Labor Day

Saturday, they had a parade and partied.
We closed the blinds and watched

Different Strokes.
Sunday, they burned their god.

We said the blessing over leftovers.
Monday, they left town.

We exhaled
the first clouds of the season.

Looking both ways, we crept
across the divide to inspect the ashes.

on the pearl river bridge
for Mack Charles Parker

the only thing they left behind
was my blood on the mattress

an alibi is worth the lint in your pocket
an accusation is as good as dead

the jingle of the sheriff's keys
in his relentless hand

men in hoods men in masks
men in guns men in clubs

a downpour
i fought like it mattered

felt my mother's hands as they dragged me
felt our bloodline running through her fingers

like a leash leading me back to my cell
the concrete swallows my blood

the universe becomes a tunnel
spurning the blackness of their eyes

cigarette holes burned
into white masks

in the back of the car they hiss
my fate into my ear

under the green rusted arms
of the pearl river bridge

no one is innocent
steady on fingers

how many shots does it take
the water licked its lips

it only takes a second for night to go black

The Healing Room

sits on top of Prayer Mountain
it isn't really a mountain
just a hill
in a land marked
by flatness
by steadiness
but it's the highest point
of elevation in this area

it is early
soft tendrils of sun
most hopeful
like a rightful childhood
scripted so smoothly
you believe
this is the way
things should be

the gazebo where we wed
stands in the center
of this postcard worthy scene
overlooking the lake and the city

a playground
wooded and canopied
yellow, green, and red
stands despite being unused

a red fire hydrant stands firmly
in the thin space where the road
meets the strip of grassy plain
just in case

the memory of unplanned burning
at the side of the highway
during much hotter months
remains in the peripheral

I swore I'd never come back

after

on the radio,
they speak of Fidel's death

in Little Havana Miami
people banged pots and pans
celebrating the end
of oppression

the morning clouds gather
in protection

a cross at the top of the gazebo
sits heavily on the roof

I can't seem to process you
as I should

who would
place faith
in the control
of a dictator?

only the desperate
you think
but are too polite
to say

remember
it only took a dozen
men to start a revolution

small enough
to do without
but enough

in the healing room
all of this matters
because this is real

Fidel is dead

and in this version of the dream
those who risk everything
to love you
will only later risk everything
to escape you

the history of nowhere
For West Dallas

say we shuffled without power
before the bridge to nowhere rose to power
before the belmont's unobstructed access
to the nation's second most beautiful skyline
came into question
before reunion tower
learned to signify
say the divorce of disruption
say the devil of an argument
say where to reposition
those outhouse natives
when the west levies widened
they were washed down the trinity
before it could overflow
hope mortgaged each spring
at the height of each season
when foreclosure slips
bloom like magnolias on front doors

Divination

my father is a black hole of questions
consuming all possible answers

i read his calloused palms
deliberate over life and love lines

roadways interrupted by cracks of skin
as if construction has been abandoned

i am proud of my spooned hands
shovels as dumb and as clumsy as his

a legacy of knuckles in this limitless childhood
and meaty fists holding god's vengeance

that will one day retreat like roadkill
barely escaping the blare of headlights

dilated pupils stretched to the edge of irises
what is the limit of a cloud of locusts

descending on the comfort food that needs to slide
down your throat like unwanted advice

or the truth, a clinking fork on an empty plate
the fizz of flattening soda is deafening

Everyone has a father

It's corduroy and turtleneck weather. Great pumpkin sun blankets afternoon. Foliage has on its primal palate. Brake lit reds. Raw marigolds. Greens smoothly aging before melting to confetti browns. We are on the school bus headed to the city. The windows are moving Monets. The girl next to me turns and asks, *Who is your father?*

On the school bus in the city, weather is raw. Each passing pothole confettis the great sun. The city is a primal palate. Skyscraping walls. Buckled sidewalks. Rush hour grays melt to brake lit reds. *I don't have a father.*

The bus has on its primal palate. Passing sidewalks rush by. In the city, the brake lit sun turtlenecks the afternoon. Skyscraping walls melt to windows. The girl next to me strums corduroyed legs like acoustic guitars. *Everyone has a father.*

Fruit

we closed our petals to make fists
a leftover sliver of moon
doubles our shadows

intention signifies
the distance between sound and light
if the mind is a gentle thunderstorm

then a threat is as beautiful
as dusk lips pressing hard into night
the way your lover does

when he wants to get him some
as a black boy in a hoodie
going home for dinner

as the fingers of a bruise
blackening into a plum after
your man beats your ass

as the click of an officer's safety
ticking like a single second
instead of opening

as the doorknob turning on itself like a snitch
you'll live by the skin of your eye teeth
 to be innocent

you were indicted before you were born
if the order of adjectives determines your net worth
then i am dead broke until the end of the month

my therapist tells me to breath
but i think that bitch is lying
this is not a costume

or a theatre of indignities
or a silent movie
my father wears gold dentures

lies are less vulgar than truth
there will always be bystanders
to collect the teeth of ornaments

hanging from dead trees
hunger is the first vital sign
o how sweet the fruit

To want to fish

Closet.   The closet is a guillotine. My hand, a sentenced witch.
When is Ma coming home?

Fat.   Fat is solid. I dog whimper. Fat is strong. Older cousin
Mutley laughs. He doesn't know the game is over. Fat is the reason Mutley
gets to fish with Gramps. His whole weight is on the jamb. Mutley is a fat boy.
This is what it means to be strong.

Plates.   Nanny erects towers of collard greens onto Mutley's plate.
When I ask for more, she says my eyes are bigger than my stomach, and hands
me a plate with reservoir-wide spaces. Buoyed between side and entree, I want
to fish. Big mouth bass. Mutley thinks I'm still playing, and presses on. Nanny
finally hears me. She frees my hand from the sharp door edges. Pink under
dermis exposed, but nothing appears broken. Breath settles into lopsided,
hiccups.

Knuckles.   Nanny shrouds my knuckles in frozen peas. Little girl, this
is what it means to be. Sun fall. Nanny harvesting Gramps's leather belt. Tide
rise. Mutleys metastasized' howls. Skin tested. Ozone shrinking.

Heels.   I dig my heels into the mustard carpet. When is Ma coming
home? My eyes are bigger than my stomach. I want to fish.

Eyes.   Mutley's eyes double diameter.   Sirened saucers. Our
redbrick apartment shudders. Labored inspiration. Bronchial viscosity.
Mutley swallows Sisyphean sized air-boulders whole. Nanny rings her
epiglottis. *Hushup now! Ya hear? Fo I really give ya suttin tah cry bout!* Mutley
has eyes. Eyes are starting blocks for summer drunk junebugs. Too wet. Too
heavy. Too stupid to fly. Old-man swaggering half-lives. Wet memory. The
mustard carpet is a mass grave for what our eyes have lost.

Stomach.   Mutley has stomach. Mutley gags. Time slows to operatic
soprano. Mutley's stomach. Bigger than eyes.

Carpet.   Mutley retches. Fingers, frozen pea numb. Redbrick.
Apartment shudders. The mustard carpet is a mass grave for what his stomach
has lost. For Nanny, fishing isn't a game. She's tackle boxed her whole life. Ma
is home. Here eyes are bigger than her stomach. She wants to fish.

Hands.   You need hands to fish. Closet. *I have hands. Fat. Mutley has hands. Plates. Ma has hands. Knuckles. Nanny has hands. Heels. Justice has hands. Eyes. We are home. Stomach. You are always bigger than eyes. Closet. I finally hear Nanny across the reservoir-wide space of time. Guillotine. We are innocent Redbrick. You are no longer buoyed between eyes and stomach. Frozen Peas. She is free. Wet memory. Shroud her tested skin. Carpet. This is what it means to want to fish when God wants you to fly.*

The Fisherman

"Ah was born in nineteen-ee-leh-ben,"
Gramps always said
before proudly proclaiming
that he and Lincoln shared a birthday
as if there were a link
between him and freedom,
or between a freedman
and a free man.

He was never able to manage
my complicated syllables
or even the short transition
between the R and V
of my shortened version.
So he called me "Reyab,"
adding an audible curve
that neither my mother nor I
could have imagined.

His liaison sharply contrasted
my guarded phonemes
with definite beginnings,
foreseeable endings,
hardened consonants
and noncommittal vowels

Every weekend he'd load up
his wood paneled station wagon
Liverwurst and Wonder bread for us
Hog-head cheese for him and Nanny
Tackle boxes, lines, and floats
Bait, hooks, and finally
-us.

We'd head for "The Rez-eh-bwor"
He'd drive and we'd watch
the shrinking rectangular prisms
of Hartford's unremarkable skyline
slowly recede, like an aging hairline
first from sight,
then from memory.

Lineage

A body once inside a body, converted
to fortune that my mother will pluck

from her neck for either me
or my brother to proudly clasp

between greasy fingers. It is more satisfying
to break something than to bury it with honor.

A riot does not need a neighborhood
to justify violence. A mouth divided,

is a former country with nail beds bitten down to the quick.
The right hand, as it waves to the wrong one

argues when there is too much or too little.
We wash our hands under the tap,

discard bare bones
on top of the kitchen trash.

I am afraid to say *I love you* because
a lure can be mistaken for a life preserver.

There is always a river, some sort of baptism,
a fracture of body and spirit. I will one day wade

until I am no longer afraid of the water or the fish.
My grandfather will cast a line and wait for me to bite.

my sister's sweater

she pulls out two cardigans
each a different shade of cotton candy
i guess i'll return these, she says

it is the day before my sister's funeral
and my mother is making sense of
the belongings that stayed behind

like vapor clinging to glass
when the neglected temperature drops
slipping away like something lost

a civil war sparked by
a dropped vase sprawling
across the floor like vomit

in her hands, she mourns
for the first time i am afraid for her
more than i am afraid of her

i'll take the green one, i say
i want unbury her
like an involuntary memory

to find a statue without arms
in the debris trailing her exit
my mother takes my offering

passes me my sister's gift
an unworn hand-me-down
a crucifix to hang around my neck

closing arguments

when conviction becomes an answer to prayers
listen for a siren's too-late warning
shotgun casings reverting glass to sand
children's earliest memories of dynamite
the riots will come like rain or folded arms

chins will be propped by knuckles
or children siced by dogs
can you see the white dressed girls
in the bathroom
their skirts belling out like tornadoes

conjoined arms wrapping around mother's thighs
like bowed presents under a tree
hot-combed hair pressed against skulls
eyelashes, earlobes, fingernails
desegregated from the torso

everyone lost their eyes in this staged killing
the neighborhood rained on itself like confetti
historical proofs w/o equations to isolate variables
the president wanted to wage peace
but who has ever turned down an opportunity for war

shut up fo' I give you suttin' to cry about
for James Baldwin

after a belted ass whooping
the mandated sharp intakes of air
either mowed to the carpet
or shaken in the glass figurines

a night's worth of humiliation on the loveseat
is a freedom rider just trying to keep himself together
closed fists and shit kickers
fire hoses pissing all over the avenues

windows and bodies bewildered
the time is now and you can't carry me
if I can't carry you
bent knees hang over a forearm

as if dipping feet into a river
we cut down the signifiers
so hollywood could direct us
to be kind to negroes

300 years of enslavement
100 years of alleged freedom
the matriarch, the noble savage enduring
time to cut down the streamers

I can't take the apathy of washington anymore
or children in cages under biceps and thumbs
you can live without your head
you just have to find another way to breathe

all spiders make webs

years are rush hour drivers
traffic thickened to mercury
guardrails standing dumbly

pressed tire and asphalt
as if they never belonged
the stories crawled out of the esophagus

your chest is a burning fist
more sensual than lips
four arms, four legs, foresight

the gate isn't as desired as the door
so why do the dead always come back?
dead is supposed to be a closed window

a car exhausting itself in the garage
this doesn't explain your childhood
or why the Italian flag runs down the center of Franklin Ave

or why falling in love with the wrong person
is a jog that never ends
as if a leash reaches the heavens

when a woman becomes unclasped
like a snapped bra she hits the ground and
the sky forgets her name

while dead men continue speaking
we should all celebrate headstones
by wearing half-masks

apocalyptic mediocracy

dead hunger
the center of gravity of all things

there are never enough zombies
acutely alive appendages

a body always leaves a stain
when the fields have been ravaged

and no thought is left to harvest
the suitcases have been unpacked

knotted gourds vomit their orange guts
all over the plantation

the last legs of a white picket fence
pray like pointed fingertips

you should touch something hollow before
stealing your neighbor's election signs

feed your family
feed yourself

feed your enemy's likeness
to a flag corps of wildflowers

standing for the national anthem
this is what it means to be legally black

to sing from every mountain top
to every broken kneecap

sing from everybody came
to every execution

sing!

we die pretty

broken signs freeze gas prices
halted neon begs to be exploited

a marriage to a closed economy
flags flex ideology

like dead skin that won't let go
slapping the wind as if

alternating between cutting
and being cut off

a fallen bumper points to
a factory's open mouth

an assembly line on the closed
shoulder of this covert war

monuments for lost battles
like the dorsal side of bone

an education breeding estrangement
an umbilical cord wrapped around necks

It gets tighter
the government issues vegan cheese

instead of passports
your mother prays for a grandchild

you pray for a bigger paycheck
in a world that says you deserve

light dimmers and filtered air
middle seats and shared armrests

the inside stomachs and forced landings
everyone isn't meant to fly

Job wasn't meant to prosper
he was meant to have faith

you deserve carbonation
paved roads and laughter

two storied cottages
and wallpaper bouquets

you deserve to exhale
without accusation

how many fallen does it take
before the tax collector notices